EMPOWER
YOUR JOURNEY

A PROSTATE CANCER GUIDEBOOK

ELIZABETH JORDAN

with **DANIEL JORDAN SR.,** *Cancer Survivor*

WRITERS REPUBLIC L.L.C.
515 Summit Ave. Unit R1
Union City, NJ 07087, USA

Website: *www.writersrepublic.com*
Hotline: *1-877-656-6838*
Email: *info@writersrepublic.com*

Ordering Information:
Quantity sales. Special discounts are available on quantity purchases by corporations, associations, and others. For details, contact the publisher at the address above.

Library of Congress Control Number: 2024904798
ISBN-13:   979-8-89100-599-0   [Paperback Edition]
                     979-8-89100-600-3   [Hardback Edition]
                     979-8-89100-598-3   [Digital Edition]

Rev. date: 12/04/2024

As you peacefully wake

may amber light flood your room,

producing beautiful sparkling light

as diamond dust all around you

To give you a gift from heaven

to create a wonderful day

filled with love and laughter

Author: Elizabeth Jordan

8-11-23 @ 2:11 a.m.

Marquis Who's Who

Elizabeth Shores-Jordan

On June 7, 2024, Elizabeth
was induced into the
Marquis Who's Who in America
for her excellence in Modeling, Photography,
volunteering with Big Cat Sanctuaries & Zoo's
for over 25 years and her books using her own
life experiences to try and
help other's. Elizabeth
will be listed in the 2025 issue of
the Marquis Who's Who book.

Dedications

First of all I dedicate this book to my husband, Daniel, who had the courage to make it through everything associated with Prostate Cancer and choose to share his story to help other men. It is in no way easy, but with a laughing attitude we made it through.

Mark Shellnut, when Daniel & I married you stood in for my dad & presented me to Daniel. I chose you to stand up for me and be beside me during the ceremony. That gesture means the world to me. You have always been a friend & we are always here for you. We love you Mark.

Sally Rhine Feather, Susan Freeman and the entire group of the Rhine Institute of Duke University for their positivity and love through the entire process.

Dr. Hollis Sigman (Columbus, GA) - Thank you for being a loving and kind doctor under such a scary situation. You allowed me to be with Daniel every step of the way and that means the world to us. You and your staff are very special people.

Dr. Henry Ngo (Columbus, GA) - Thank you for being a great and kind doctor and checking Daniel's blood work so thoroughly. Without you, we would have never known Daniel's PSA were so high. You saved his life by being a great doctor.

EXTRA Special Thanks to my mom, dad and Hannah. Even though they are all in heaven, Daniel could feel my mom's hand on his shoulder during the surgery and radiation treatment. She calmed him because she knew the fear. She went through radiation treatment three times for breast cancer. During surgery, Daniel felt Hannah lying next to him as he drifted off under anesthesia. We have seen enough to know that angels are all around us. Especially when we need them.

Introduction

In the scheme of things, we are here for such a short time. In my experience, it seems there are those who fight, those who ride the difficulties of life out and those who give up under the pressure. My Husband and I have always chosen to tackle any situation head on. That is exactly what we chose to do when Daniel was diagnosed with prostate cancer in February 2023. We chose to tackle cancer head on with a bit of comical flair. We live our lives with the mentality of we can either laugh and make it through the situation or cry and fall apart. Medical professionals everywhere will tell you laughter makes all the difference when it comes to healing. Stress tends to inhibit the healing process. The Amos Cancer Center in Columbus, GA will also tell you a great attitude will make things so much easier on your health when dealing with a horrible diagnosis. With my degrees in Psychology, human behavior and biology, I was able to help Daniel project a positive lighthearted attitude through out what we were going through with the diagnosis. The word CANCER, is like an immediate slap in the face.

This is the journey of my husband's fight using what we call "Blissful Ignorance" and humor to survive a prostate cancer diagnosis. We hope our story helps those going through a cancer diagnosis while using a light prospective as we did to deal with our own diagnosis. We want to alert men of all ages to have their PSA numbers checked through a simple blood test. This can catch a diagnosis of prostate cancer extremely early and save lives. We also hope by sharing our story that we can shed a little bit of light on cancer survivor's and the struggle of dealing with the diagnosis along with the caretakers. We offer our love and support to anyone who has been diagnosed, surviving cancer and the care giver's helping their loved ones struggle through Cancer. It is a hard job, but you are everything to those you support and love through the process.

Daniel and I have set up an email where you can reach us for support, encouragement or to ask any questions you may have during your journey. As a psychologist I offer guidance through "Angel Heart Guidance". You may contact either of us free of charge at: <u>angelheartguidance@gmail.com</u>

Please place "cancer" in the subject line.

Our Terms

1. **Unobtainium** – Something you cannot obtain or possess.
2. **Blissfully Ignorant** – You know what is happening but choose not to worry about it in the here and now. No need to worry until a doctor has confirmed.
3. **Taint** – The perineum or the area between the testicles and the rectum. You will hear this term a lot from urologists.
4. **Erectile Disillusionment** – We were told prostate cancer would cause ED, but it has been opposite for us. We're not sure if we are subconsciously using sex to deal with the stress of the diagnosis or if having a positive attitude has brought us closer.
5. **Pitiful Piddles** – When your urine stream is not normal. It creates a dribble effect that causes you to urinate every 10 minutes or so.

Chapter 1

The Unknown

As a psychologist, I feel if either of us tackled the diagnosis with a negative attitude or looked at the cancer diagnosis as a death sentence, it would have been so much harder on both of us. Some people close to us thought we were not taking the diagnosis seriously, but we truly were. We chose a different way to handle it using a positive attitude. You heal so much faster with a positive attitude. Whether you're the patient or the care giver, please remember that statement.

Daniel and I were married in November of 2018. He was a past smoker, but has now been smoke free for over 6 years. Neither of us were much of a drinker and that's one vice we never had to deal with overcoming. We try to eat healthy, exercise, drink a ton of water daily to defeat dehydration and also for anti-aging to extend a healthy outcome. When we were smacked in the face with a cancer diagnosis, we felt like the axis to our world had been removed and gravity no longer existed. Our lives, our thoughts were spinning out of control. It proves no matter what we think we never have total control over our lives and bodies.

We had been seeing a family physician who did the very minimum for his patients. We decided to change to a new doctor and this proved to be a life changing decision. On October 10, 2022, we chose Dr. Henry Ngo as our family physician. He told us he would like to do extensive blood work to see how everything was with our health. He did this with all of his new patients.

On December 14, 2022, Dr. Ngo was concerned because Daniel's white blood count was high (it was high with my mom before her cancer was found) and tried to pass it off in our heads as a scratch wound from our cats that had not healed. His PSA number was 14.7 and little did we know that the PSA is your prostate number. This number should be around 0.1 or it can be as high as 0.4 according to your age. Dr. Ngo referred Daniel to a urologist in Columbus, GA.

On January 31, 2023, Daniel's urologist checked Daniel's PSA through a urinalysis & blood test and the result was 17.8. Just a head's up, we did not know that if you have marital relations before a PSA test that your numbers are higher. We told Daniel's urologist, we made love the night before and asked if the blood work could be repeated. He decided to bring us back in two weeks later with instructions to not touch each other the night before. The numbers were 14.7 at the next blood test. Daniel's urologist told us this could indicate prostate cancer. We felt like we had both been kicked in the head as the "C" word crossed his lips. We were not expecting to hear the word cancer and we were horrified.

Daniel's urologist scheduled a prostate biopsy for February 6, 2023. I have been through a breast biopsy and I assured him they would probably give him some sort of a numbing agent in the area or something for pain. I tried to ease Daniel's mind, but I had no idea what he was in for with this delicate procedure.

He was prescribed one 5mg Valium and antibiotics to take before the procedure. Daniel's urologist allowed me to be in the room during the procedure to comfort Daniel. We walked into the procedure room and the nurse told him to disrobe and get on the table. She did not offer him a gown or give him a sheet to put around him. He was told to walk 6 feet to the table bare ass naked with twig and berries swinging in the breeze. We looked at each other, thinking this is not going to be a good day.

We knew the procedure would be ultrasound guided, but we thought the ultrasound would be placed on top of the skin to view the prostate. It became apparent very quickly we were wrong. The ultrasound wand looked like a huge dildo with a condom on it. It appeared to be 2" in diameter and 8-9" long with blue lube on the top drizzling down. Daniel had no idea what the ultrasound guided wand looked like and I was not going to be the bearer of bad news at that moment. Then I saw the same machine they used during my breast biopsy- "oh No" I screamed in my head.

The nurse draped a paper sheet over Daniel as Daniel's urologist came through the door. He told us the procedure would take about 8 minutes and would be only a bit uncomfortable.

Daniel's urologist asked Daniel to pull his knees into his chest and began to insert the ultrasound probe into his anus. Daniel squeezed my hand so hard I was bruised, but at that moment, I was ok with it. In the same area the biopsy gun was inserted. When Daniel's urologist pulled the trigger on the biopsy gun it shot a needle through the rectal wall into the prostate to snatch out pieces of prostate tissue. With every loud click the biopsy gun made, I had a flashback from my own breast biopsy.

We thought there would be four biopsies, but at number four, Daniel's urologist told us we are half way through. We looked at each other and said "Holy Hell". The last 4 were the most brutal. At that point I was holding Daniel's head next to my chest with all my strength. He was experiencing so much pain that his eyes would roll back in his head as he passed out. Tears were running down my face because I did not know how to help him. I believe that is one time I saw True Honest Fear in his eyes. The pain he was feeling was killing me inside.

When it was finally over I was still holding his head against my chest as hard as I could. I couldn't let him go. Daniel's urologist told him that most guys hop off the table, walk it off and go back to work. If so, they are a hell of a stronger person than Daniel and I thought we were at this moment. After about 5 minutes, it was just Daniel and I in the room. I helped him to sit up and as I did, I noticed fresh blood running down the ultrasound probe. Seeing my husband's blood made my heart drop and I became very concerned. I asked the nurse if he needed gauze or something to put in his underwear to keep him from bleeding to death. She answered no, but I was very concerned. The nurse told us he must urinate before he could go home. I walked in the bathroom with him to make sure he was ok. When he urinated, it was all blood. It horrified both of us. After having your ass snatched out 8 times and seeing so much blood it is a scary thing to see. The areas snatched out of the prostate was bleeding and coming through the urinary tract.

We headed home with no medication to help Daniel. I told Daniel not to worry, I had something at home in case he needed a tablet for pain. As I helped him into bed he began to explain his discomfort and pain to me. He was having cramps similar to what women know as menstrual cramps. I told him a heating pad would help and it did help with the cramps. Every time he urinated he was seeing blood and he told me he felt like he had been kicked in the nards. At one point, he had to pull a blood clot from his twig while urinating. It horrified him, but the doctor told us it was normal. This went on for a few days, but staying in bed, resting and caring for his symptoms the best we could made it a little easier.

During the recovery time he was given instructions such as not to lift anything heavy because it could cause bleeding. I tried to help as much as I could, but men are stubborn. I tried to do things to keep him from bending over and doing too much too soon. I didn't want any negative outcome as a result of being too active too quickly. Within a few days he was able to take a ride and we visited his parents. They were happy to see him because it was the first time since the biopsy surgery. It was relief and sadness on their face. After all, we were still waiting for the results of the biopsy. It was a tense time and we were all praying for the best, but secretly begging God to allow the results to be negative for cancer.

I would like to add a suggestion, the biopsy procedure can be performed under anesthesia at the hospital. We were told it was a simply biopsy with minimal pain. We would highly suggest that you choose to have a biopsy performed at the hospital under anesthesia and not in the doctor's office. The results are the same, but it is not worth the horrendous pain to go about it with no drugs to help out. It is one of the most horrible procedures I have ever seen a man go through. Trust me, YOU WANT ANESTHESIA FOR THIS PROCEDURE and insurance will pay for it to be performed in a hospital setting. If Daniel ever has to go through a prostate biopsy again, we will have it performed in a hospital. Daniel went through 8 biopsies, but I have heard of men having up to 16 taken at one time.

I also recommend checking the reviews of the doctor when you are referred to a urologist. The first one we were referred to had horrible reviews and we chose to use the urologist that Daniel's dad has trusted for years. You want the best you can find in your area.

Chapter 2

Biopsy Results

February 10, 2023, I opened my email to see the biopsy results from Labcorp. I know from my mom's experience with breast cancer that cancer cells show up pink. With anxiety and fear in my heart I read the results line by line. I wanted to be sure not to miss anything. I felt a dagger in my heart as I read the word "carcinoma". OMG, I thought, how was I going to keep it together to tell Daniel the news with optimism? I wanted him to know this isn't a death sentence and treatment is where we need to go from here. A few lines down the page, I saw the images of the pink cells. There it was, the cells such a pretty shade of pink. How can the pretty pink cells be something so horrifying? It is like a total short circuit wave to my mind.

I read the report three times before I discussed it with Daniel. I looked at Daniel pushing back tears, fear and the nightmare he was dreading. I had to be his rock and his optimistic wife, friend, love and not show my own fear. I was terrified myself, but I had to look him in the eyes and appear fearless at this moment. I took a deep breathe, turned to him and with a fractured smile, I told him I received the biopsy results. A look of fear came over his face that I have only seen during the biopsy itself. I started to read the report as it was not so bad at the beginning. His gaze beamed at me as I read the word carcinoma. His eyes began to fill with tears as I fought back my own tears. It is Carcinoma which can be cured and doesn't spread like Metastasises cancer. That's a good thing, I told him as I took his hand. I turned the report to him to show the images. The cancer is only on the left 1/3 of the prostate, the center is precancerous and the last part is cancer free. This is a good thing. It has not spread. We can handle this and go through treatment. We will be fine as I looked in his eyes as tears begin to fill my eyes.

We both felt like we had been kicked in the chest. We prayed for the results to be negative. We convinced ourselves it was just a mistake at the lab and not cancer. We were wrong. As I held him in my arms and tried to comfort him, my mind was spinning. I didn't want to think about the possibility of losing him to cancer. I would not lose him after it took us 46 years to find each other.

I clasped my hands on each side of his face and looked him in the eyes. We are fighters, we have fought our entire life to be where we are now. We will fight this, I told him with confidence on my face and in my voice. His expression changed as he knew I was correct. We will fight this together and win. Just as we have before, understand, I told him. He shook his head yes and hugged me like never before. We will see Daniel's urologist in a few days and he will tell us what we need to do. We will do exactly that and take care of it, ok? Yes, he shook his head.

I told him, we will continue to practice "ignorant blissfulness" until we speak to Daniel's urologist. We will not spend our time on worrisome thoughts until then. We will enjoy each other's company and live our life without missing a beat, ok? Yes, he shook his head, as his confidence came back knowing he was not alone dealing with this.

After we grasp the concept a bit in our own minds, I phoned Daniels parents to tell them the results. Daniel couldn't speak about it and I placed the phone on speaker. I asked his mom to do the same because I couldn't repeat it to mom and dad separately. I only had the strength for the word cancer to pass my lips once.

I could hear the clinch in their voice, the concern, and the tears as I told them the results. Although, they couldn't hide their fears and tears either, they both told us to wait and see what Daniel's urologist told us about the report. His mom told us to pray and they would do the same until we see the doctor. They were both as devastated as we were at the moment. It was a shock to everyone. We never expected it to really be a cancer diagnosis.

We asked his parents to keep it quiet for the moment. We needed time to wrap our heads around this and deal with it together before we could tell anyone else. We needed to speak to the doctor and know exactly what was going on before we told the devastating news to anyone else.

We tend to deal with things internally. We would tell the brother's when we were ready, but certain members of the family we did not want to know anything about what we were dealing with at the moment. It seems there is always someone in the family who chooses not to be part of your life. We both feel if they chose not to be in our lives, then we do not need their pity when they think their family member may die. This is one area we were imminent about controlling ourselves. Only those who chose to want to be in our lives would know what truly was going on with the situation. No matter what other's try to tell you, it is ultimately YOUR decision on who you tell, when you tell them and if you even decide to let them know at all. Do NOT let anyone manipulate you into telling people that choose to not be a part of your life. This is your life and your diagnosis, you have the right to handle it the way you see best for yourself and your spouse. This is not the time for any people or family members to be involved who couldn't give a damn on any other regular day. YOU are in CONTROL!

Chapter 3

Daniel's urologist's biopsy review

It was February 17 when we walked in Daniel's urologist's office feeling numb. We had no idea what he would tell us we needed to do to move forward. We both knew once we met with the doctor there was no going back. The diagnosis was real and we had to take care of the situation.

We sat in the exam room holding hands with tears in our eyes. There were no words spoken between us verbally as Daniel's urologist walked in and sat down. He had a serious look on his face as he took a deep breathe before speaking. I squeezed Daniels hand to comfort him. We both knew what he was going to say, but we didn't know how serious the treatment would be to make it to the other side.

Daniel's urologist told us it was cancer, but it was caught extremely early. He told us he did not want to discuss treatment at this point. He asked Daniel to have a bone scan and a CT scan to show him more details. The scans will show whether the cells have spread outside the prostate and to make sure it had not spread to his bones. These two test would determine the severity of the cancer and the treatment, Daniel's urologist told us.

We walked out of the office feeling sick. As if knowing for the first time. It was official now, it was cancer.

After leaving Daniel's urologist's office, we drove to Daniel's parents' home. Daniel could not speak of it and asked me to tell his parents what the doctor told us. As I began to tell them, their eyes filled with tears. I was trying to get through everything we had just learned without falling apart myself, but it was extremely hard. I was trying to stay on a positive note, being as upbeat as possible and telling them we had a lot of options for treatment. Blissfully Ignorant is what we chose to be and we would portray that in front of others. A united strong front is what we would show. Nothing less than strength and optimism.

Daniel's mom asked about telling the family and I told her that our decision was to keep it to ourselves for the moment. We would tell those we wanted to know when we thought it was time. We needed to deal with this personally inside our marriage before we could tell anyone else. We were struggling to wrap our minds around this at the moment and we needed time to do so. We demanded for it to be that way. It was the only way we could handle the diagnosis and that was by having some sort of control over the situation.

Chapter 4

Starting to tell other's

We decided to tell Daniel's older brother, Jay. As Daniel started to tell him the diagnosis, he handed me the phone and could not speak. I finished telling Jay what we had learned, as I heard the same clinch in his voice as we heard before. He was upset and told us he would call us back. Jay took it hard and called back later that night to tell Daniel he would be by his side through the entire process. Two brother's so entwined at this moment was something I will never forget.

Daniel called his younger brother, David. As Daniel told him the news, the line became silent. David told him he would call him back when he could think of something funny to say to lighten the mood. It took him two weeks to process that his brother had cancer and think of something to say to Daniel.

We never knew how emotionally exhausting it would be telling the family. We knew it was on their mind that they could lose Daniel, just as it hindered our minds with the possibility. In private, we had times where we fell apart and cried together. We were trying to keep a good attitude until we knew more, but it was consistently in the back of our minds.

We were portraying "Blissful Ignorance" especially in front of Daniel's parents. The first few times we visited his parents after the diagnosis was really difficult. We could hear the catch in their voice and see tears in their eyes. Sometimes we had to cut the visits short to try and contain our own emotions. We were emotionally healthier in the company of each other. We chose to carry on with life normally and not waste a moment in worry.

We both love music and have always used it to get us through the hard times. Each morning we would play our favorite videos and songs to start our day. The music put us in a great mood and that made all the difference to us mentally. We chose bands and artist such as Adam Lambert, Queen, Sam Smith, Danger Danger, George Michael and Winger to name a few. Adam Lambert's personality, over the top costumes and general happiness in his eyes was energizing to us. Sam Smith being his infectious self was so entertaining and upbeat. George Michael's song, "White Light", took on an entire new meaning for us. We saw the video for the song before as what

George was going through at the moment when he found out he was sick, but now we were going through the same things he spoke of in the lyrics when he was sick.

We would binge watch Marilyn Monroe and Elvis Presley movies. There is no way you can be unhappy while watching Elvis and Marilyn on screen. We both grew up with our parents listening to Elvis and it holds great memories in our hearts. It seems to take us back to child hood when listening to him.

The time waiting for the next step was excruciating. At this time, we were spending some of our time getting familiar with treatment options. We were positive recovery was 100% at this point from our research. We refused to entertain any negativity from anyone. The research was very clear and we still chose to be blissfully ignorant of any negative outcome.

Chapter 5

The Tests

On March 1, Daniel was scheduled for the bone scan to see if the cancer cells had spread to his bones. We were a bit worried because of the $150 up-front co-pay. At the moment, we could not pay the amount and the test wouldn't be performed without the payment. We chose to keep the appointment and see if there was any way around the co-pay. We were not going to allow a co-pay to stand in the way of Daniel's health. The test must be completed for Daniel's urologist to proceed with treatment options.

We arrived at the hospital and were checked in by a sweet lady named Vivian. We asked her if we could pay $25 towards the co-pay and be billed for the remaining. Of course, Vivian told us. As we finished the paperwork and started to head out of her office, Vivian asked if we had cashapp. Yes, we responded, but we were a bit confused. We had paid the $25 in cash. She asked for me to write down the cashapp account name for her. Looking at her confused, I wrote it down and handed it to her. She escorted us to the door and said, by the way, I transferred $25 from my personal account to your cashapp card. Why, I asked her, because I can, she replied. We can't accept that we told her. She replied, it's already done.

The bible speaks of angels being put in your path when you need them most. At that moment, we believe Vivian was one of those angels. We needed her love and support as we moved to the next stage of the tests. We felt vulnerable and alone at that moment. She told us to do something good for someone else and that's how we could pay her back. We both thanked her with tears in our eyes as we hugged her. She saw how emotional we were and her loving nature made us feel like we were not alone at that moment.

We proceeded to the bone scan both speechless. I was allowed in the room with Daniel during the scan. It created a calmer atmosphere for both of us. I didn't want him to be taken from me for a moment. I wanted to be by his side to comfort him.

Next was the CT Scan to pin point the exact location of the cancer cells in the prostate. It was also needed to see if the cells had spread to the glands or other nearby areas. This would help determine the path of treatment.

The CT scan involved radiation, therefore, I wasn't allowed in the room. I kissed Daniel as he pulled his hand out of mine to follow the nurse. I was sitting alone in a small area waiting for him to come back to me. I found myself worrying about the outcome and near tears. I was so focused on Daniel that nothing around me registered in my mind. Until I heard a horrendous scream like someone was being tortured. It immediately jerked me from my own thoughts. It made my blood curdle with fear while a man screamed. I felt a panic attack coming on just as the nurse brought Daniel back to me. I asked her what was happening to that man. The nurse told us he was having a very painful bone biopsy. I asked couldn't he be given something for pain and she replied, no. To be sure the biopsy was taken from the correct area, the man must be aware. We left with a sinking feeling in our hearts and in tears for the unknown man. Our concern for our own problems had shifted to an unknown man that we will never forget.

After such an emotional day, lack of sleep and the stress of the situation, we fell asleep as soon as we arrived home. Knowing the tests were over and having the support of Daniels family created a sense of peace for the moment as we were finally able to sleep peacefully for the first time since the diagnosis.

Chapter 6

The Next Step

It was three weeks before we saw Daniel's urologist for the results of the bone scan and CT scan. Our blissful ignorance took over once again. We spent our days watching movies and cuddling in bed. At times, Daniel would become quiet and distant. It was a total mood change and I knew something was wrong. I tried to speak to him about it, but he wouldn't tell me what was going on in his head. I knew he was worried and we were trying our best to make it through together, but at times his mood would change abruptly. I felt like at these times I didn't know how to comfort him or tell him it would be ok. All I could do was hold him tightly and not say a word.

When we finally received the scan results, it revealed his cancer had not spread beyond his prostate. His glands, nearby tissue and bones were clear. This was such wonderful news, but to hear the treatment options was overwhelming.

We knew from this point on that no matter what treatment option we chose, we would have a lot to deal with going forward.

It seemed a number of options were available such as surgery to remove the entire prostate, hormone therapy to reduce the level of testosterone in his body, radiation therapy, brachytherapy or a brand new therapy called Proton therapy. Daniel's urologist told us to think about it and the decision was ours. He would help us with our decision, but with Daniel he could choose any option available.

We began to research each type of treatment to obtain the knowledge to be able to make a calculated decision when the time was at hand. Of course, being next to my mom as she underwent radiation therapy three times for breast cancer had given me a bit of knowledge. Hormone therapy could be used in combination with radiation therapy if needed. Testosterone feeds cancer cells and the shots bring down the testosterone level.

Brachytherapy consist of radioactive wires being inserted into the taint under anesthesia before radiation. The wires would be inserted to target radiation therapy into a certain area. The wires would stick out the body a few inches during the radiation. You would then be taken from the hospital to the cancer clinic by ambulance. After the radiation therapy, the wires would be removed when you returned to the hospital. This is known as internal radiation therapy. In addition to this, radioactive seeds would be placed into the prostate and remain in place. The seeds would omit radiation for a few months to deteriorate the cancer cells. There are 2 surgeries to place the wires before radiation therapy. This treatment requires less radiation therapy treatments and is recommended for prostate cancer that has not spread to the lymph nodes or other parts of the body.

Proton therapy is offered in Atlanta, GA and a clinic in Florida. It is said to be easier on the body than radiation, but the number of treatments really doesn't change very much. We would also need to drive to Atlanta each day or check into a hotel. We have two kitties at home and didn't want to leave them for a week at a time. We also wanted the comfort of home while going through this.

Even knowing there are so many treatments available and Daniel was a great candidate to be cured of this disease, it was scary as hell looking forward.

We were patiently waiting to see the oncologist two weeks later at the John B. Amos Cancer Center in Columbus, GA. Upon seeing Daniel's oncologist, we will know which treatment he thinks is best. The treatments all seem horrible and we were both freaking out and nervous trying to decide what to do. We both felt like we were at a mental point of exploding. Our minds were reeling and sleep was not our friend at the moment.

We continued to binge watch TV shows to keep our minds busy, but at times worry took over and I couldn't tell you what the movie I was watching was about anymore. I could tell Daniel was experiencing the same mental discomfort as every other cancer patient. It is hard to imagine something in your body that you have no control over. You are at the mercy of the next doctor visit or the next step. We felt so vulnerable and at a loss.

We both started having nightmares and waking up screaming. The fear of the unknown is horrible and it affects you even in your sleep. I tried to be a comfort for Daniel, but at times it is so overwhelming that I feel I can't do enough to help him. My heart felt like I had been stabbed with daggers. All I could do was pray the treatments would not be as scary and painful as it seemed at this point. I tried to ease Daniel's mind by telling him my mom experienced no pain during radiation therapy. I was trying to calm Daniels mind by telling him mom felt no pain during radiation. I feel until a patient experiences the first treatment it's hard for them to believe it's painless. I knew Daniel believed me, but fear still consumed his thoughts. It was exhausting for her to make the appointments each and every day. To her, that was the worst part of that radiation treatment option.

Chapter 7

The Oncologist

On April 10, we saw Daniel's oncologist for the first time. He told us Daniel had stage 2B prostate cancer that had not spread. We listened to the treatment options once again and Daniel's oncologist felt 6 weeks of radiation therapy would be Daniel's best choice. He explained he would have surgery before radiation started to insert 3 gold seed markers into the prostate. The seeds will navigate where the radiation would be emitted. Space Oar gel would also be placed between the prostate and other organs to prevent damage to those areas during radiation. In the past, radiation therapy would melt tissue to each other and create problems of its own. Daniel's oncologist's had created the Space Oar Gel to protect the other organs from this happening. He pulled a small pouch from his pocket and showed us the gel. It was clear and looked a bit like thick hair gel. He explained, the radiation will not penetrate the gel and it makes for better recovery and a better healing experience for the patient.

We left the oncologist office in a mental haze. The conversation in the car was silent on the way home. We were both in our heads dealing with thoughts and fears of what we had just heard. The diagnosis, the treatment options were very emotional, stressful and mentally draining.

At times, I felt like I was screaming inside my head trying to deal with what was to come. I knew Daniel was going through the same thing when he would walk outside to sit a moment. The silence of the day, the warmth of the sun and the sound of the birds seemed to comfort Daniel mentally in a way that sometimes I couldn't. I knew when he needed me he would come back to me. At times, we needed to be alone with just our thoughts and no other distractions. We gave each other the space to deal separately and it made us stronger when we came back together. I tried not to break down in front of Daniel. Although, I was horrified cancer would take him from me. At times, I would run a bath to relax and break down in the tub while I was alone. I had to have time to release my emotions so I could put my brave face on to encourage Daniel that everything would be ok. I never once let him know that I was afraid of losing him to this disease, but in my mind, I was horrified.

∽ *Chapter 8* ∾
The Surgery Date

We received a call on April 26, 2023 stating the surgery had been set for May 25, 2023. At this time, the 3 gold seed markers and the Space Oar Gel would be placed in the proper place. We were also told about 2-3 weeks after the surgery radiation therapy would begin. This is to give the prostate time to heal a bit and for Daniel to recover from the surgery before moving on to the next step.

Daniel had been waiting for the phone call to find out the date of the surgery, but the weekend after knowing when it was scheduled was extremely difficult. He had been really down and maybe a bit depressed. I understood because surgery is a scary thing to most people. Daniel and I are a lot alike. I had rather be told the surgery is a few days away, instead of having it on my mind for a month. Daniel was apprehensive about undergoing anesthesia and I was horrified something might go wrong and I could lose him.

It was like impending doom was a month away and it consumed our thoughts. A month is a long time to worry about fear of the unknown.

We were having a really hard time and it seemed Daniel wasn't himself. It also seemed everyone around us was showing a less than positive attitude. I really didn't understand the rude things people were saying and the negative emotions they were projecting towards us. It seemed overnight to turn from tears and concern to rude remarks and this was the time when we did not need to hear negativity. It was really hard on me trying to keep Daniel positive with the negative vibes around me.

On the morning of May 8, 2023, I woke up to Daniel screaming in his sleep. I woke him up and he was extremely upset and in a panicked state. I made him sit up in bed and drink a bit of water. I asked if he wanted to talk about the dream he was having when I woke him. He told me he had dreamed about the upcoming surgery and in his dream he died. When I was finally able to wake him completely and calm him down, he noticed something. He told me in the dream his watched stopped when he died. He looked down at his watch and it had really stopped. He began asking questions that I could not answer. Especially when the day before, the battery had been replaced with a brand new one. He also asked me if it was possible a negative spirit or entity could enter his soul during anesthesia. I told him I could not answer these questions, but I had a friend who know the answers.

When I woke the next morning, I immediately sent an email to Sally Rhine Feather at the Rhine Institute located at Duke University in Durham, NC. I first met Sally about 25 years earlier. Her father started the Rhine Institute for Parapsychological studies and she has been over it for many years. The Rhine Institute studies phenomenon that can't be explained. Sally is a brilliant lady and I knew she would know the answers.

I told her about Daniel's dream and about his watch stopping. I know I have a high energy field around me because a new watch battery that is guaranteed to last a year, will only last about 2 months on me. The energy in my body drains the battery. Sally told me that Daniel probably has a high energy field within his body as well. She told me that stress coupled with such an intense dream of that magnitude can produce enormous energy while dreaming and drain the battery. She knew of other's who had intense dreams of that magnitude and woke with their watch batteries drained as well.

She recommended for me to contact a group at the Rhine Institute who were testing energy's healing ability. A group of parapsychologists were conducting studies to try and help people. The group led by Susan Freeman would gather in sessions and focus their positive energy and prayers on healing those who volunteer for the study. We believe positivity and prayers always help and Daniel decided to participate in the study. We filled out the volunteer paperwork and sent it back to Susan.

On May 11, 2023, we decided to go mother's day shopping. It would have been the 22nd birthday of my Canadian Lynx named Hannah. I lost her at 18 years old in 2018. She was my heart, my child and when she passed in my arms it was one of the hardest moments of our lives. I raised her from a 4 week old cub and I missed her so. We thought spending the day shopping would take our minds off all the stress of the day.

We had a really great day and neither of us had cancer on our mind that day. In the past few days, Daniel had been feeling tired, weak, and lightheaded. We knew the symptoms of cancer would show up, but we didn't know when or where. While we were out shopping Daniel told me he felt really well. Better than he had felt in several days.

The next day, I sent an email to Susan Freeman at the Rhine Institute. She is over the energy healing group we were participating in. I told her about the great day we had the day before. It was the first time Daniel had felt that well since the diagnosis. We both felt a sense of peace in our minds for once. Susan told me that

Daniel and I were included in the healing session on May 10 for the first time since he volunteered. I was blown away. I believe god created the energies in our bodies and in the universe. In my own psychological studies, I found positive mind sets and attitudes put forth positive energy into the world. I feel the energy healing is a form of prayer and positive energy and positivity can never hurt.

So far, I'm very impressed in the group. We had no idea Daniel would be included in a session that quickly, but we both feel it is helping.

Chapter 9

Fear Consumed US

We were getting things ready for Mother's day to celebrate with Daniel's mom. I handed the card to him to write her a note and as I was about to write my note, I realized what Daniel had written to his mom. It stopped me in my tracks as I read what he wrote to her. He told her that if anything happened to him during the surgery, the treatment or due to the cancer in general that he wanted his parents to promise him something. He asked them to continue to treat me like a daughter and not abandon me.

As I read this, I was in tears. He told me there is a special section in his journal for me in case something happens to him. I don't want him to feel this way going into surgery. I have been trying to tell him that it should be easily completed because he will not require any incisions. As hard as I tried to tell him everything would be ok, I was trying to convince myself of the same thing. I was also afraid of losing him.

As I tried to soothe his fears, I could hear echo's in my own mind of the same fears.

Being diagnosed with cancer, looking at surgery, anesthesia, radiation therapy was so much to go through. Things can always go wrong even with the best doctor's. My worries mimicked his, but I had to push them aside and assure him that he was in the hands of the best doctor's. I told him they would take great care of him because they are the top in their field.

As the surgery date grew closer and closer I knew Daniel was nervous. He showed me the journal he had written a special section in for me, but he also added a section for his parents and his brothers. It was a way of leaving last words just in case he wasn't able to tell us goodbye. I promised him I would be sure they would read what he had written in case of the worst outcome. As I promised this to him, tears streamed down my face and the entire conversation made my heart hurt. I didn't want to lose him. This has been such an emotional period to go through and Daniel had never faced anything like cancer before. It brings your own mortality to the forefront of your mind.

In the next days leading up to surgery we were both physically and mentally exhausted. Sleep eluded us due to the fear of the unknown and the fear of the outcome.

I started having stress induced migraines again. I haven't dealt with them in over ten years, but they can be totally debilitating. I think after the surgery is over we will both feel a lot better. At this point the surgery and especially the anesthesia is the scariest part for both of us. Daniel is 6'5 and a big guy. I know the anesthesiologist are great at their jobs, but I hope they can put him under anesthesia enough without over dosing him. Even with Daniel being a corpsman in the Navy and medical knowledge, it is completely different when you are the one being put under by strangers.

One of the most stressful and exhausting aspects of going through all of this has been the need to keep reassuring his family that Daniel will be ok. We couldn't tell them that we were scared too. We had to be the rock to hold everything together when in the presence of other's.

In private we would cry together when it all became too much to handle, pray together for the strength we needed to get through the surgery and the radiation. At times, we would turn the TV off and cuddle together in bed to comfort each other. The silence helped us to reconnect with each other and give each other strength.

Chapter 10

Preparing for Surgery

The day before surgery, we met with Daniel's urologist to discuss the procedures and go over any concerns or questions we may have. We understood everything at this point because we had researched everything and asked a lot of questions.

The next stop was pre-op check in at the hospital. They drew blood, performed an EKG and went over all the necessary information such as not eating after midnight and which of his medication he could take the morning of the surgery. As we were leaving the hospital, we were told to stop by the Amos Cancer Center to pick up the gold seed markers that would be used in the surgery. It didn't seem like an unreasonable request and we agreed. We were told to keep them safe, do not leave them in the car because it was 100 degrees and do not bend them.

ON the way to the Amos Center, we were thinking it would be 3 small seeds of gold in a small container that would fit nicely in my handbag. They would be easy to keep safe and not be forgotten the day of surgery because I always have my bag with me.

We arrived at the Amos Center and told the receptionist why we were there. An oncology nurse came out and handed me 3 steel needles 20" in length. Each were individually wrapped in a plastic packaging. I asked her, what are these? She explained the needles would be inserted in the taint in three areas and the seeds would be shot out of the long needle into the prostate to mark the edges of where the cancer cells were located. We looked at her like she was speaking an alien language. They looked horrifying. As our gaze met over me holding the needles we both had a look of horror on our face. I don't think either of us heard a word the nurse told us after laying our eyes on the needles. We were not ready to see that and I feel the hospital or the doctor should be responsible for picking the needles and seeds up. A patient does not need to see that when they are already nervous about what is going to happen. It created a sense of panic between both of us.

The night before the surgery we did not sleep at all. We had to be at the hospital at 1:30 p.m. Even though we did not need to be at the hospital early, it was almost like we wanted to spend what might be our last night together conscious. We watched TV and tried to occupy our minds, but the fear of the surgery and the metal needles rang through our thoughts.

Below are the photos of the needles we were asked to pick up from the Amos Cancer Center. These will be inserted into the taint and used to place the seeds in the prostate.

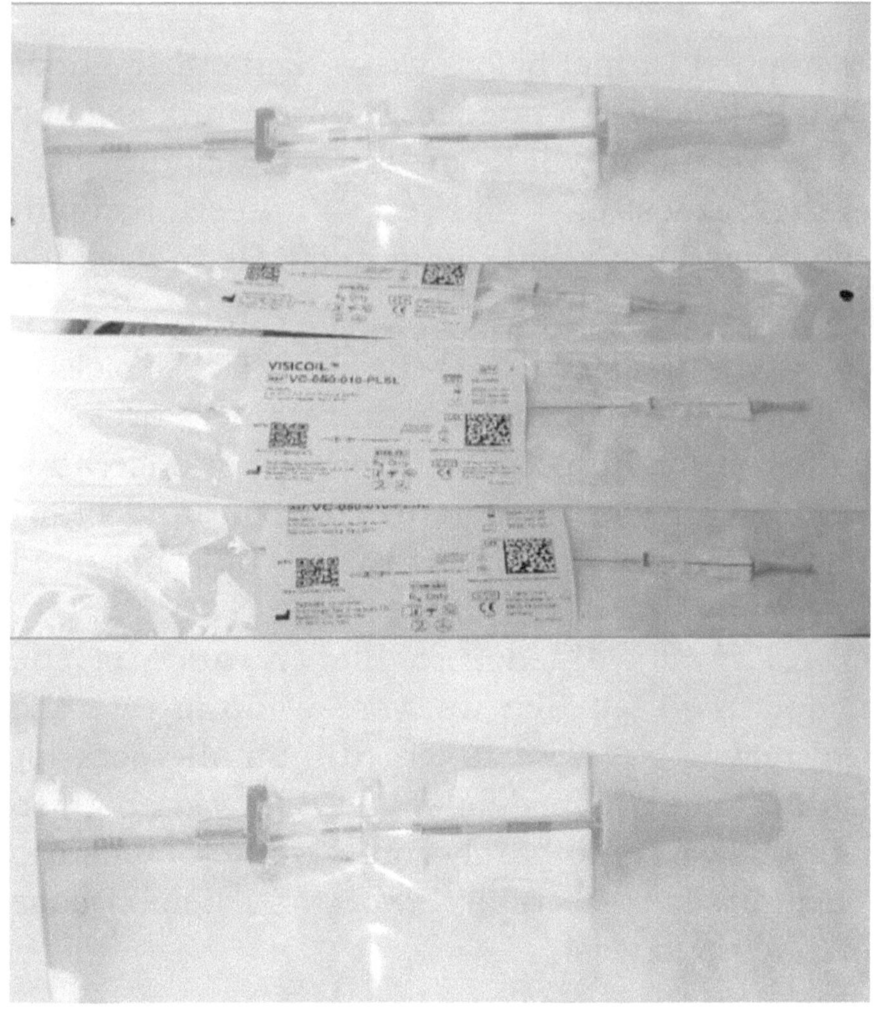

Chapter 11

The Surgery

I stopped Daniel before we walked out the door and gave him a huge hug. Everything is going to be ok and it will be over in a few hours. This is the hardest part and you will breeze through radiation. Only good thought, ok. He hugged me tightly as we left home.

Our first stop was at the pharmacy to pick up antibiotics and oxycodone that Daniel's urologist called in for him. I knew from experience after surgery all you want is to go home and crawl into your comfy bed. This way I would not need to stop again.

As we walked into the entrance of the hospital we felt like we were walking into the unknown. We were taken to a small room for Daniel to be prepped for surgery. We were both so nervous we could barely contain our composure. The nurses were really sweet and helped ease our nervousness.

Daniel hates IV's and the nurse was having problems getting it put in correctly. I leaned over and kissed him as she put the IV in once again. It helped to calm him during the painfulness of inserting the needle. Next the anesthesiologist came in to speak with us. After he left, one of the nurses told us he was over the Anesthesia department. She told us he was the very best we could have been given. That made us feel so much better. Next, Daniel's urologist stopped by to check on both of us. Daniel's urologist told us it would not take very long and he would not need any incisions. It would only be insertion of the long needles in three places to implant the 3 gold seeds and the Space Oar Gel would be ultrasound guided to protect his other organs. I asked Daniel's urologist what the chances of the cancer returning to his prostate after all the treatment is finished. He told us it will be gone. We felt so much better after speaking to the doctor's.

Daniel had to be cognitive to speak to the doctor's and sign the papers to allow the procedures, but after that was completed the nurse was able to give him something for his anxiety. She told him it was a liquid version of Xanax. She also gave him several medication for nausea. One medication surprised me. She gave him 2 Benadryl, I never knew Benadryl would help with nausea. She told him sometimes people vomit after anesthesia and they try their very best to stop that from happening.

Daniel had been so anxious and stressed, but after the first shot of liquid Xanax he calmed down. He told me it felt like a wave washing over him with calmness. If only they could have given me something for my anxiety, I would have felt a lot better too. I could tell he was mentally feeling better and that was a relief to me.

I was sitting on the edge of his bed and he couldn't seem to keep his hands off me. I knew he was feeling much better at that moment. Every time he would reach for me the machine would scream like a banshee. After the third time the nurse came in to stop the machine, she asked what was going on. I told her he was trying to get frisky. She looked at Daniel and told him, you are feeling more relaxed my dear. She was giggling as she walked out of the room.

We finally had a few moments alone before the surgery was to begin. I reached in my pocket and pulled out a heart I had cut from red construction paper and handed it to Daniel. On the heart, I had written "I love you and I will be with you". I told him to take it with him and I would watch over him. He had the heart in his hand the entire time.

When the surgery nurses arrived, I had tears in my eyes as they started to take him to surgery. One nurse noticed and grabbed my hand. She smiled at me and said we will take great care of him and she promised me she would bring him back to me safely. Just the possibility of him being under anesthesia horrified me. I didn't want that to be the last time I ever saw him. I told him I loved him as they started to take him away from me. Daniel grabbed my hand and saw the tears in my eyes. He told me, "It's nice to be loved so much by someone". I told him to remember to tell me that when he returned.

I walked back into the tiny room with fear in my heart, tears in my eyes and prayers running through my head. It took me a few minutes to compose myself enough to call his parents and Jay to let them know Daniel had been taken back to surgery. I couldn't show fear in my voice because that is not how I handle things. Everyone was still emotional and worried although I put on a strong front.

I was told the surgery would be about 20 minutes with 90 minutes in the recovery room. After 45 minutes, he was back in the room with me. I have never felt such relief as when the nurses brought him back to me. He was wide eyed and so happy to see me. The nurse told me she had never seen anything like it before. He was in recovery 15 minutes and woke up with three questions – "What happened, where's my wife, and I need to pee."

The nurses wanted him to eat a few crackers and drink a little soda before he left. She told him he also needed to pee before he could leave. Daniel told her I have needed to do that since I woke up. She led him across the hall to the restroom and told me she has never seen anyone recover so quickly and ready to go home. His surgery was scheduled for 3:30 p.m. and by 4:45 p.m. we were able to leave the hospital.

We stopped for take out on the way home. The ride was a bit uncomfortable because he was very sore from the procedure. Once we made it home and finished our take out, I settled him in bed. I asked him how he felt and he said he felt like he had been violated. When they say ultrasound guided, it is not placed on your stomach. It placed inside the anus and causes a lot of pain and bleeding. I gave him his pain medication and started him on the antibiotics after he had food on his stomach. The oxycodone helped with the pain a lot more than we thought it would and the pain subsided a lot.

I think tonight we will finally be able to rest since the surgery is over. Since the initial diagnosis in February, we have not had a peaceful night sleep. We have both had nightmares, been awake with worry and our hearts and minds in tangles for fear of the unknown to come. Tonight, we can finally breathe a sigh of relief, thank God for letting us make it this far and finally rest.

After the surgery

I thought things had been going well since the surgery, but the night of June 1st things changed with Daniel. He told me I needed to stop treating him like his mother. I had been pampering him and making sure he didn't pick up anything he shouldn't to prevent injury or bleeding. We wanted the surgery to be a success and not lead to additional bleeding, scar tissue or adverse reaction because of something we did incorrectly.

It seemed after the anesthesia, Daniel became hostile for a period. He was saying things which were very hurtful to me. I didn't understand what was happening. The worst part is over and radiation will be painless. I was curious whether the reality of cancer being real had finally hit Daniel. I know from experience that when someone is going through a devastating event they seem to take it out on those closest to them. In my mind, I knew it was because I was the one closest to him. In my heart, I was hurt and spent time crying when I was alone. I tried not to argue with him, but I did express the things he was saying was hurtful. He didn't understand why I felt that way. Later, he told me he didn't remember saying the hurtful things to me. I also found out later that anesthesia can cause some people to be hostile. It all depends on how it effects the body and everyone is different when it comes to the results.

This was one of the hardest times for me. I always am aware of things I say especially in an argument. Whether you mean what you say or not, it cannot be taken back. Criticisms will always be in your partners head and they cannot be erased. I tried explaining to Daniel that whether he meant the things he said or not, they cannot be taken back. Forgiveness can always be given, but in the back of your partners mind, the echo of the words you said are always there.

I learned a very long time ago to be careful what you say even in arguments. I never want to hurt anyone I love on purpose. Whether you're the cancer patient or the care giver, I feel this is a very important lesson I can pass on to everyone.

Chapter 13

Getting Ready for Radiation Therapy

On June 12, Daniel had his first appointment to start radiation therapy. When we arrived at the cancer center, I took a photo of the "Hope Bell" and the plaque that sits beside it. Upon completion of radiation therapy patients ring the bell in a ceremony and the team gives them a certificate of completion. It is a celebration and everyone in the waiting room at the time is part of the blessed event. I wanted to share the photo of the bell with Daniel's parents and brother's. I tried to keep them involved as much as possible. I didn't realize how emotional it would be for me to see the bell again. I was with my mom when she rang the bell three times. It took me directly back to the celebration of her being cancer free and brought tears to my eyes. What a lovely memory of being there with her, but also sadness because I missed her so much.

Before Daniel went back for the CT scan, I drew a heart on his thumb. It came out looking more like angel wings. I told him maybe my mom was guiding my hand and sent the wings to let him know she would be with him.

At the first visit, the team performed a CT scan to locate the 3 gold seed markers. Once located, they placed circle markers on his skin above where the seeds were placed. He had three marks on his skin. One on his left hip, one on his right hip and one on his lower abdomen. This is where the radiation will be targeted to treat the prostate. I was given extra markers in case one came off in the shower. I would place it back on top of the marking they made with a sharpie marker. I was a bit nervous about this because I wanted to be sure I knew the exact area to replace the sticker. I took a black sharpie and drew a line all the way around the round sticker they used to mark the seeds. The black mark stayed in the shower even when the clear sticker would come off. It made it very easy for me to keep it aligned perfectly as it was supposed to be.

We were told once treatment started he would have 30 treatments for 6 weeks. It would be 5 days a week with Saturday and Sunday off to rest. His radiation team will now map his treatment with Daniel's oncologist and call us when the treatments are to start.

After we left, Daniel told me he became very nervous during the CT scan. He closed his eyes and tried to clear his mind, but he said he felt a warmness on his right shoulder. It seemed to calm him down. He said the weird thing was that I had drawn the heart/wings on his right thumb. He asked me if it was possible my mom had her hand on his shoulder to calm him. Anything is possible I told him. I believe in angels and so does Daniel. We both feel mom guided him through the radiation and helped calm him because she knew all too well what it was like to go through it.

We returned home that night and Daniel had a sense of peace. The team told Daniel the radiation therapy would feel exactly like the CT scan. In his mind, that was a huge comfort. Things had been so very stressful between us that our love life wasn't the same. For the first time since the surgery, we made love that night. I don't know if it was dealing with so many emotions and stress, but it was different. It was very mental, very emotional, very moving and very spiritual. It was something neither of us have ever experienced before. It was like reaching a higher plain of intimacy.

The markings were a cross with a plastic waterproof circle on top. I drew the marks out beyond the center marks so when I needed to replace a marker, I knew the exact spot to place it.

I also drew a circle around the clear sticker to be exact.

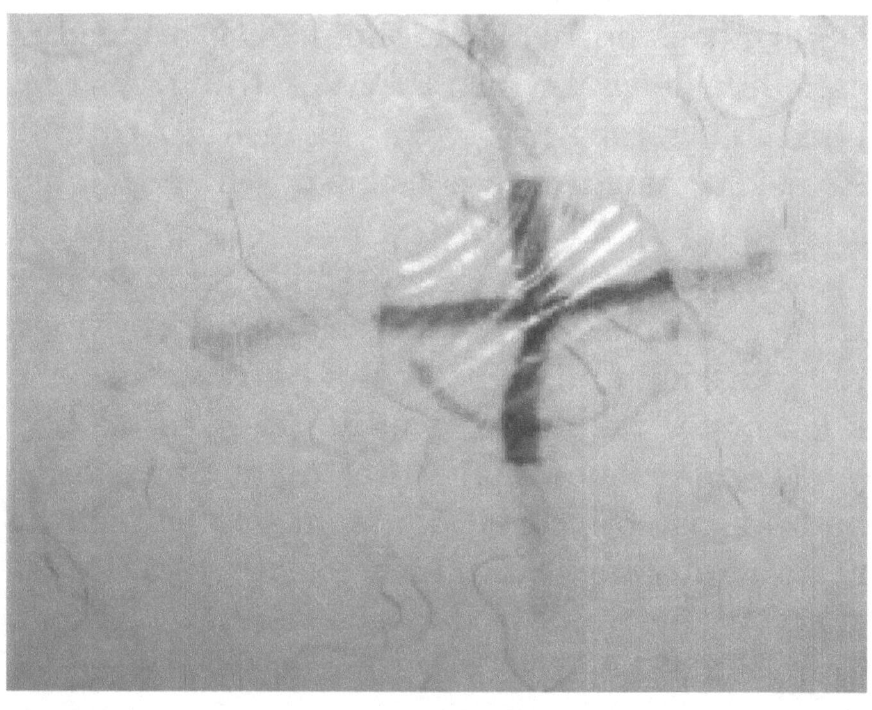

Chapter 14

Once Again Waiting

It seems there is a lot of waiting to go from one stage of being diagnosed to the testing and then waiting for the next step. It was June 22 when we were notified the first radiation treatment would be June 26. We both had been waiting for the call because we knew the sooner treatment started the sooner it would be finished. I thought Daniel would be happy to finally have a date for the first treatment. After he was off the phone with the cancer center he told me the date of the first treatment. I immediately wrote it down in my daily calendar. As I was writing it down, Daniel became upset with me. He looked at me and said, "You could tell me it is going to be ok". I was shocked and speechless. It will be ok, I told him. Instead of looking at the appointment date as one step closer to the end, he became very upset and it led to an argument. I told him I knew he was nervous and the treatments will be over before he knew it. I reminded him that if my mother can make it through at 70 years old with no problems that he can do. He was a lot younger than my mom was when she went through radiation.

It seemed that since the call with the radiation start date everything has caused an argument. I tried my best to keep calm. I knew his emotions and fears were getting to him, but with him on my case about everything it was causing me to have tremendous migraine and stress headaches.

After 3 full days of arguing and crying it seemed I couldn't do anything correctly. The migraines are becoming worse and debilitating. I was at the end of my rope and I realized cancer wasn't only hard on Daniel, but it was also very hard on me. I was trying my damnest with everything in my power to make the entire process as easy as possible. I'm not looking forward to driving to the cancer center every single day for 6 weeks either, but I didn't complain about it. It is a means to an end and the cure for the disease. I know he is angry because he has cancer, but I didn't have anything to do with him having it. I don't understand all the anger all the time.

I went so many nights without sleeping and each day was the same. Daniel was angry, I was crying and it seems everyone around us who knew was in a vicious mood. I happened to be the one who received the blunt of the anger. Maybe it was because I was just the one there and it was directed at me. I know he is angry, afraid and worried. My heart is aching with all the negativity around me, but all I can do is try to be strong, supportive and always on Daniel's side through this.

Chapter 15

Starting Radiation Therapy

The morning of June 26 I was still awake at 2a.m. I found myself looking towards the heaven's talking to my mom. I asked her to please be with Daniel as he goes through his first radiation treatment in a few hours. I told her, that Daniel needed her wisdom and love to be with him during the treatment. I prayed to God to please be with Daniel and guide him through the first treatment and allow the experience to help relax him through the next 29 treatments.

As we left for the appointment, Daniel started an argument with me in the car. When we arrived at the Cancer Center, I was crying. The oncologist nurse who called Daniel back must have noticed I was upset. A few minutes later Daniel's oncologist appeared at the door and called me back. He escorted me to a small exam room and asked if I was ok. I told him since Daniel had received the call for the first treatment he has been really angry and hostile.

He asked if Daniel had been physical with me in his anger. I told him no, never. He told me some men become very angry and aggressive towards their spouses and family members. He mentioned that Daniel was a big guy and he wanted to make sure I was ok and I was safe. HE told me he would continue to check on me as well as Daniel and if I needed to speak to him, he was there for me as well. Daniel's oncologist's was so sweet and his concern made me feel like I had someone on my side. After speaking to him I felt much better knowing this is something a lot of men go through.

After the first treatment, he didn't say a word to me on the way home. He was still angry and I thought maybe he didn't want me with him at his appointments. Maybe it would be easier if I stayed home. Maybe I was causing more stress than comfort.

I could look into Daniel's eyes and I couldn't see him. I saw anger and I didn't understand the change. Is he simply mad at the world because of his cancer? Am I not doing enough to support him? I simply didn't know. All I knew was at this point I felt like sitting in a corner and crying. What do I need to do to help him? Is there even a way I can help him at this point? I was simply exhausted from arguing with Daniel and the negativity I was receiving from some of those close to us at this point left me where my tears burned my skin.

Each Monday we see Daniel's oncologist, Daniel's oncologist. When Daniel was called back for treatment #5 today, the nurse called me back also. She took me to a small waiting room and told me Daniel's oncologist knew things were going badly and that I was upset. She told me that Daniel's oncologist was worried about me. He wanted to speak to me alone before Daniel finished his treatment for the day. I told him Daniel was still angry. He asked if it was still anger through words only. I told him yes, just words. Daniel's oncologist told me he had been worried about our emotional state since he and I spoke before. I told Daniel's oncologist that Daniel and I had an intense conversation about the treatment and it helped the situation. I told him he could either accept what was happening, complete the radiation and come through it cancer free or stop the treatment and die. After the first treatment, he did admit it did not hurt. He said it was more mental than anything because all you hear is the machine making clicking noises and it's a bit spooky in the room by himself.

As Daniel's oncologist left the room, the nurse escorted Daniel into the room where I was sitting. As Daniel entered the room he actually had a smile on his face. Daniel's oncologist told us he was happy to see a smile for once. I told

Daniel's oncologist we were in a better place mentally. We had an intense conversation about the treatment and it helped the situation. We told Daniel's oncologist we had sex for the first time since surgery and it was amazing, but we wanted to make sure we couldn't rupture something or dislodge the seeds. No, he said with a giggle, sex is great for stress relief and it will help mentally also.

Daniel's oncologist told us Daniel's entire prostate is being radiated at 250 rppms. This is causing the healthy tissue to swell. The swelling causes pain, pressure and bloating similar to menstrual cramps. He told us it will also cause digestive issues.

During the 5th treatment Daniel started sweating on his forehead. Before we made it home it had caused a breakout on his face at every spot he had been sweating. It was the radiation seeping through his pores. We started taking a small bottle of facial toner and cotton rounds with us. After each treatment, he would use the toner in the car on his face and this stopped the break outs.

Daniel found out another side effect around treatment #10 was pain when sneezing. He told me that when he sneezed it felt like he had been kicked in the nards. Daniel's oncologist looked at Daniel really seriously and told him not to sneeze. Of course, we all laughed. Thank goodness Daniel's oncologist can have a sense of humor with us because it made the situation a lot better.

One of the worst parts of the treatments were getting up at 8a.m. Neither of us are morning people, but we made it each and every morning. After the treatments, we would come home and take a nap. The treatments made Daniel tired and it really helped us to get through.

Daniel mentioned to the staff that the worst part was lying on the table listening to the machine. His oncology nurse told him she could remedy that and as she entered the booth to start the treatment she turned on the radio. She also told him that he is never alone because they have camera's watching him and can speak to him through a microphone and he can speak to them anytime he needs to. All of these things helped to ease his mind and helped him to not feel so alone.

Chapter 16

Side Effects of Radiation

I feel the radiation treatments are interfering with Daniel's hormone levels. As a woman, we all know how it feels when our hormones are being disrupted and irregular. I'm definitely not a stranger to hormones being out of balance. Daniel has started experiencing symptoms that all women are familiar with such as hot flashes, night sweats and overall sweating that comes out of nowhere. This is indicative of hormone imbalance such as women deal with during their periods and during menopause. This is a side effect some men experience during radiation therapy.

Other symptoms he experienced was what he called "soft Serve" when dealing with bowel movements, constipation, "pitiful piddles" or feeling like you need to urinate, but only piddling. This is caused by the Space Oar Gel and the swollen prostate pressing on the bladder. After each treatment, he is excessively tired. All of these symptoms was expressed by his oncologist, but he also has nightmares. It seems not every patient has nightmares, but I wanted to mention it in case you experience this symptom.

When we saw Daniel's oncologist the next week, we asked him about the side effects. He told us the Space Oar Gel and the swelling of the prostate during radiation causes pressure on the bladder and creates the piddles. It is similar to a baby pressing on the bladder during pregnancy causing a women to urinate more frequently.

The oncologist also told Daniel to use Mylanta to control the constipation, but to use Imodium A-D to control diarrhea. Daniel soon learned when to take a sip of which one to keep things flowing normally. It is experimentation, but you can reach a controlled medium using both.

The Pitiful Piddles would keep Daniel up all night long needing to go to the bathroom every 15 minutes, but we found that AZO taken about 5 p.m. helped him to sleep throughout the night. Taking 2 tablets helped extremely well and it can be bought off the shelf at any store like Walgreens, Walmart, etc. It is natural and made with cranberry juice to help the kidneys and bladder.

I also asked Daniel's oncologist a question that had been on my mind. I wanted to know once the cancer cells were destroyed what would replace them in the prostate. Daniel's oncologist told me that where healthy cells were in the prostate that healthy cells would grow back, but the cancer cells would die and be replaced with scar tissue. We were told the cancer cells would not grow back especially because the cells were carcinoma.

During my research, I found the rules of thirds. I asked Daniel's oncologist about this and he explained to me that this deals with the number of cancer treatments and where you are during treatments. At treatment number 10, Daniel is 1/3 of the way through treatment. At treatment number 20 he will be 2/3 through treatment and at the last 10 treatments he will be at the 3/3 point. What this means is at the 2/3 completion the cancer cells are dead. They continue with the last 10 treatments or the 3/3 point for good measures to make sure all cancer cells are dead.

I also asked how long it would take for Daniels PSA numbers to be normal. Daniel's oncologist told us in 12-18 months after treatment the PSA number should be around 1. Of course, each person is different and sometimes 3 months after the last radiation treatment the numbers can drop significantly.

Around July 12, the anger with Daniel has subsided and have been replaced with side effects from radiation. All we can do at this point is laugh at the side effects. It's either laugh or cry and we chose to laugh. That is how we came up with terms like "Pitiful Piddles" and "Soft Serve" for diarrhea. After finding the balance with Mylanta and Imodium A.D., Daniel was much more comfortable. The skin toner helped a lot with the break outs from radiation on his face. The only side effects we couldn't control was the hot flashes. After experiencing the side effects he's been going through, Daniel said he had a new respect for what women deal with in their lives.

With each sneeze it caused Daniel to double over and he said he felt like he had been kicked in the nards. At times, all I could do was laugh and he jokingly told me that was adding insult to injury. I felt helpless because that was one side effect I couldn't do anything to help him with and he understood my laughter was the only way to deal with it. Of course, after the pain subsided he would laugh too because it was after all a bit funny. Daniel said that was one hell of a side effect to go through.

With the soreness in his under carriage area from sneezing and from swelling caused by the radiation, he was worried about how an orgasm would feel. He was afraid it would be an excruciating pain and we decided to take things really slowly.

Things were more normal when we were alone and at night while watching TV in bed, I would lay my head on his lap. I had to be really careful not to put pressure on his stomach because of the swelling, soreness and sensitivity of his prostate. The healthy cells would swell when being radiated and it was visible through his abdomen. At this point, the heating pad helped with the cramping as it did before. While going through this the doctor's do not give pain medication. All I could do is use the heating pad and Tylenol or Advil to help with the pain. We found that by taking one rapid release Tylenol and one liquid gel Advil it seemed to help a lot better. It can be the generic version of Tylenol and Advil also. They work just as well and will save you a little money.

Chapter 17

How Others Were Dealing With the Situation

It seemed those around us were not dealing so well with what we were going through at this point. There were times when we needed support and understanding, but we received negativity. We were constantly being told about other's who were going through prostate radiation who were not having any side effects. I feel the other men were not telling the side effects they were going through to their friends. Maybe at 75 years old men were not as open as we were about what they were experiencing. Maybe they were embarrassed to tell their friends the entire story.

According to the oncologist, all men experience diarrhea, constipation, hot flashes and sometimes other side effects that Daniel didn't experience. With family members telling us their friends were not experiencing any side effects, it really didn't help us deal any better. We felt like they were seeing Daniel as weak for what he was going through and that is not what we needed to hear. It is what it is and you deal with the side effects the best way possible.

The one constant source of encouragement was Daniel's older brother, Jay. He called everyday to check on both of us. He was the only one I could speak to honestly when Daniel was angry. I could speak to Jay and the conversation was kept privately just between the two of us. That is what I needed, was someone I could trust 100%. Jay was our rock and we could never thank him enough for his love and support through the entire process. He cried with us, laughed with us and was a true brother in every sense of the word.

We met a couple at the cancer center named Mary and John Terry. They were a few years older than we were, but I feel it was fate that we met each other.

The first day we met them John was called back for his radiation treatment before Daniel. John seemed a bit nervous and after he was called back I sat down next to Mary and we introduced ourselves. John was also there for prostate cancer and I asked Mary if I could ask her about his treatments. As Daniel was called back for his treatment, Mary and I spoke like old friends. As John came around a corner after his treatment, Daniel put his hands on John's shoulders and told him "We have this my friend" and hugged him. From that moment on, we were friends with them.

Our friendship gave us someone to compare side effects with and talk about treatments. This is something we needed. Someone who was going through the same thing, the same side effects and knew exactly what we were dealing with at the moment. Each day we would see John and Mary at the cancer center. They are such great people we grew to see each other as family and love each other as family. Meeting them was one of the best things that happened to us during this process. We had companionship each morning and we supported each other. We spoke about everything that was concerning us at the moment. It was so much easier having such loving, supportive friends to help us deal with the situation.

Chapter 18

Treatment #16

On July 19 was treatment #16. We hoped as the treatments progressed the side effects would become better. Daniel was still dealing with swelling as the nerves, glands and prostate was being radiated. This was causing extreme cramps, bloating, pressure on his bladder, hot flashes, mood swings, piddling and still trying to keep his intestinal track working correctly. On top of the side effects he was feeling extremely weak and exhausted after each treatment.

Daniel's oncologist told us we could make love whenever we were ready, but with all the pain Daniel was dealing with we were both a bit nervous to try. One night Daniel came out of the bathroom with a weird look on his face. He was laughing and told me he wanted to see how painful an orgasm would be, but in case something went wrong he didn't want to try with me. He told me he could feel the sensation of an orgasm, but it was an intense pain like he's never felt before. He told me he didn't ejaculate at all and that really scared him. I listened intensely as he told me. At one point while telling me, he compared it to an episode of the cartoon Family Guy where Quagmire only had a flag come out that read "Bang" with a poof of air. At this point, all I could do was laugh hysterically. Daniel's oncologist had told us that after radiating the prostate, some men cannot ejaculate. I asked if the sensation of orgasm would be the same and Daniel's oncologist assured us it would feel the same as before. Daniel and I both agreed that as long as the sensation was the same we could deal with the lack of fluid. Daniel's oncologist also told us this condition may be temporary. Daniel was afraid I would be disappointed if the condition was long lasting. I told him, as long as he has the sensation and satisfaction of our love making the rest didn't matter. I understand as a man this would be on your mind, but a woman's perspective is different. In my eyes, this does not affect how I feel about him at all. He is the same man I married, but because of the treatment he will be with me much longer and cancer free. If we had to give up sex to save his life, I would be ok with that too. My biggest fear was losing him and I would do anything to keep him with me healthy.

If you are going through prostate cancer and worried about anything, please speak with your spouse. A loving relationship can withstand anything as long as the communication is open and honest. Never be afraid to speak to someone you love about what is on your mind. These are the things that makes a relationship long lasting. Trust in your partner and always be honest with them. I can't stress this enough.

With Daniel being exhausted from the treatments my first priority is making sure he gets the rest he needs. We are also trying to keep things as normal as possible. Although I want to do everything in my power to make this journey easy for him, sometimes I need to back off. If he feels like doing dishes or folding laundry, I don't stop him. We have always worked together on things around the house and its important to still allow him to do what he feels up to doing. I guess my nurturing nature causes me to want to do things for him, but that isn't what he needs at the moment. The more normal things can stay the better he feels.

Once a week when we leave treatment we will stop for ice cream. It is a relaxing treat for both of us and I don't think anyone can be upset while enjoying ice cream. When my mom was going through radiation, we would stop for Starbucks coffee. It's the little treats that help make the situation better to handle. There is nothing easy about dealing with cancer for the patient or the care giver, but the treats help to put a fun aspect into the day.

Chapter 19

Emotions

My mom and I spoke about everything with each other, but maybe it's been such a long time since she went through treatment that I don't remember all the emotions involved. I lost my mom in 2013 and she was 5 years cancer free when she passed.

It really hurts my heart when Daniel tells me he doesn't feel like the strong man I married in 2018. I keep reminding him this is only temporary and things will be back to normal before he knows it. I know it is difficult to be a strong person and feel so helpless with something growing inside your body that you cannot control. I had my own experience in my 30's and it is hard to wrap your mind around cancer. Daniel and I are both people who like to be in control of our lives and when there is something you have no control over it is a blow to your mental stability.

The night of July 21, I walked into the bathroom and Daniel was sitting on the edge of the tub. I kneeled down in front of him and asked if he was ok. He told me he just needed a moment and that cancer was mentally getting the best of him. He told me he was mentally and physically exhausted like he has never felt in his life. He looked at me with fear in his eyes and told me he felt like he couldn't stand up because he felt weak. He told me he was sitting there repeating in his head "stand the hell up". I tried to help him up, but he stopped me and said he had to do it himself. I wrapped my arms around him and whispered to him, you can do this. It took a few minutes, but he was able to conjure up the strength to stand on his own. I was so proud of him. He took my hand and apologized for putting me through all of this. I told him, we took each other for better or worse, sickness and health. I take my vows very seriously and at this moment it was not only his fight, but also mine against cancer.

I have tried not to break down since the treatments started. I'm afraid if I do I may not be able control myself. I'm mentally and physically exhausted just as Daniel is feeling. The mental torture is one thing people do not prepare patients for while dealing with cancer.

Chapter 20

A Nice Surprise

July 24 we met with Daniel's oncologist for our weekly visit with him. We found out Daniel's treatments are going so well he will only need to go through 28 treatments. As of today, we only have 9 treatments to go. It only eliminates 2 treatments, but what a difference it makes mentally. Although we are both exhausted, we feel a renewed sense of completion because we can now see the end. As of tomorrow's treatment Daniel will be on the 3/3 portion. All of his cancer cells should be dead at this point and the next 9 are for good measures to be sure none of the cancer cells were missed.

We left the cancer center with a renewed spirit and both in a great mood. What a sense of accomplishment we feel. I am so proud of Daniel for his strength and devotion to making it to every treatment although some days the treatments were the last thing he wanted to do.

Starting on July 27, Daniel's radiation dosage increased from 220 rppms to 350 rppms. The higher dosage will make sure all the cancer cells are dead. This is standard procedure for the best outcome possible for the patient.

At the moment, Daniel has learned how to use the medication to control his tummy issue. We are not sure what side effects will come with the higher dosage, but we are convinced we can make it through them too. It feels like we have been going through this for months, but our spirits are renewed as we move towards the last treatment in one week.

Chapter 21
The HOPE BELL Ceremony

I would think with the very last treatment coming up that Daniel would be ecstatic, but the three days before he's been in a weird mood again. It has caused arguments and once again I don't understand. He has been angry at me, but he will not tell me why. The treatments will finally be finished, but he refuses to tell me what is going on in his head.

On August 4, 2023, Daniel will complete treatment #28. His very last treatment today. Mary and John Terry walked in as Daniel was called back for the very last time. I was so happy to see them. They came to see Daniel ring the bell and to celebrate with us. The love in their eyes was something you rarely see in people any more. We exchanged phone numbers and agreed to stay in touch. After all, we had been through hell with them. We were now linked to them for life as family.

As Daniel walked out after the last treatment, his entire team of nurses came out with him. He was presented with a certificate signed by the entire staff who helped not only him, but also me to make it to this point. As Daniel rang the Hope bell, I felt the sadness that had been weighing so heavily on my heart lift. Everyone in the waiting room celebrated with us. So many had tears in their eyes just as we did each time we witnessed someone ring the bell. It is a very emotional experience even if you do not know the person ringing the bell because you know what it means to the person. I took photos because we wanted to remember the staff members who helped us through the process and the love they shared with us.

We could only have 2 guests at the Hope Bell where Daniel had received the treatment. Our two guests were Mary and John. Jay, Daniel's brother drove from Florida to Georgia to see his brother ring the Hope Bell. We had his mom, dad and Jay meet us at the Hope Bell in front of the Amos Cancer Center. That is the bell where family can gather if you have more than two members who want to attend.

On the way to the Hope Bell where his family was to meet us we decided to stop at the Hope Bell my mom had rang three times. Daniel looked to the heavens and said, "Mom this is for you" as he rang the bell in her memory.

We continued to the Hope Bell where Daniel's family was waiting for us. Jay, Daniel's mom and dad was so excited to see him ring the bell. Once again, we took photos to remember those who were there to support us throughout the process. After the Bell ceremony, Daniel's dad took the family who attended to lunch to celebrate. It was a great celebration with a sense of completion, relief and accomplishment.

Chapter 22

After the Last Treatment

On August 7, it had been three days after the last treatment. Daniel feels as if he is already passing the Space Oar Gel. It is said to stay in the position for 6 months. It will slowly be passed through urine. Daniel told me when he urinated it looked a bit like a jellyfish. Hopefully it is starting to pass to help stop the piddling. His tummy problems are much better at this point, but he is still piddling every 10 minutes or so, but the AZO is still helping with that issue. He said his stream is becoming a bit more normal. For the first time in a month or so he is starting to get an erection again.

Each time my mom finished radiation I would give her a piece of jewelry. To keep up the tradition, I found a ring online with the radiation symbol. When it arrived I gave it to Daniel and told him every time he looked at the ring it was to remind him that he was a cancer survivor. I told him how proud I was of him for completing the treatments and being so strong. He had tears in his eyes as he said he loved it and hasn't taken it off since I gave it to him.

We were told it will be 6 months since the last treatment before Daniel's body will be completely healed. We've spend a lot of time resting and watching movies. After going through treatment everyday, we are both exhausted and taking time to catch up on our rest.

August 9, we were watching America's Got Talent. A man was dancing for his mom who was dealing with breast cancer. The song he chose to dance to was "*How do I say goodbye*". I guess after being strong through the process of Daniel's treatments everything hit me with this guy dancing for his mom. I thought of my mom and what she went through, losing mom and my dad. I thought of my fear of losing Daniel when he was first diagnosed. I didn't want to even think of losing Daniel after only 5 years of marriage. Everything hit me at that moment and I began to cry like I haven't in a while. Daniel grabbed me and hugged me, I was finally able to tell him through a veil of tears how horrified I was that I would lose him. HE told me that I've hidden it extremely well from him. I felt like I needed to hide my fear because I didn't want him to think he was dying. My emotions and mental exhaustion had taken over and broken free after holding it inside for so many months.

It seems since the first argument before radiation started, things haven't been the same between Daniel and I. It's been 10 days since his last treatment and he is back to being angry. I try to comfort him, keep his mind off things and keep his spirits up, but it isn't working. I would think he would be in a great mood with radiation being over. I am mentally at my wits end trying to understand where the anger is coming from now. He tells me he doesn't understand it himself, but it breaks my heart.

Chapter 23

Weird Things Are Brewing

It's only 11 days after the last treatment and the area is still healing. Daniel still has pain of his prostate and abdominal area. The pain is coming from the swollen tissue and cramps. He is still having pain in his twig and berries. At this point, urinating is causing pain from all the area's involved. The pitiful piddles are still hanging around causing much needed bathroom breaks every 10-15 minutes.

We have come to find that if you are wanting children it may be a good idea to try and get pregnant before radiation treatment. Prostate cancer is slow growing and you would have time to try before starting your radiation treatment.

We knew after radiation it may not be possible to ejaculate, but we noticed a different problem. It seemed fluid was being produced, but not at the time of an orgasm. Daniel told me it's the damnest thing he has ever experienced and didn't understand it.

The nurses at Daniel's urologist's office (Daniel's Urologist) are the sweetest ladies I've ever met. I told him I would call and ask the professional's. We have asked the nurses crazy questions before and they laugh with us, but give us the information we need. They always tell us that our personalities are refreshing because we see humor in everything.

Daniel decided to call the nurse and put the phone on speaker so I could ask question's too. He told the nurse things haven't been in sync ever since radiation ended. She asked him to explain the situation and he told her how things seem to have a mind of their own. She began to laugh and said, "Baby that's normal". It means the nerves and healthy tissue are healing. Daniel continued to make light of the situation and she laughed hysterically. She told Daniel she was having a really rough day and really needed a great laugh at the moment.

I told the nurse that I read on the Mayo Clinic website that taking 20mg of Sildenafil (generic Viagra) will also help with healing of the nerves. She told me that is absolutely true because the low dose helps push blood through the nerves into the prostate to help heal the healthy prostate tissue faster. She placed me on hold and spoke to Daniel's urologist about prescribing a low dose. He agreed and called in the 20mg dosage to be taken 1 tablet by mouth 1time a week. This will help heal the healthy tissue, nerves and to help prevent ED problems in the future, this is something you can speak to your Urologist about prescribing for you. The nurse also mentioned the AZO for the pitiful piddles and mentioned it would help him sleep better without needing to go so many times throughout the night. Daniel told her he was still using the AZO and it had improved things tremendously. It will make the urine appear a pomegranate color, but that is normal.

September 4 was one month after the last radiation treatment. We decided to take a road trip and the pitiful piddles seem to have subsided. We rode for almost 4 hours and didn't need to stop for a bathroom break. Things are improving tremendously and more rapid than we expected.

About 3 months after the last radiation treatment, the tummy issues, piddling issues and pain have all subsided. We were told to give things 6 months after the last treatment for complete healing to occur. Daniel can feel the sense of control coming back to his undercarriage. He can tell the nerves are healing in the area. The low dose of Sildenifil (generic Viagra) seems to be helping the nerves heal a great deal faster.

At the 3 month point, things have not begun to sync up yet. We knew the radiation would save his life and we knew the potential side effects before we started treatment. We can handle the side effects we are seeing, but I could not handle the alternative of losing Daniel. We choose to laugh about the side effects Daniel is experiencing. It's the silliness that really helped us make it through the process of cancer. We found laughter to be relaxing and really helped stabilize our moods when we needed it the most.

Four Months Out Of Radiation

Daniel is still having mood swings and anger after radiation. At times, he doesn't seem like the same person as before. I try to speak to him about him, but he just gets angry. I can't figure out if it is still from having cancer or what is causing it. Is it from what he has been through? Is it possible the radiation has caused the attitude change?

Tonight he sat down with me to speak about how he feels. He finally told me that he has been experiencing confusion at times. I looked online at the Mayo website which deals with radiation side effects. Apparently, radiation can cause dementia like symptoms in some people. I feel it's better to tell him and try to help him remember things when he experiences confusions than to hide it from him. He told me it scares him with the horrible things I have told him that he has said to me in anger while going through radiation. He said, he doesn't even remember arguing with me or the cruel things he has said to me. I told him it scares me too, but I feel heartbroken too with the things he did say during the arguments. Daniel was in tears and told me he would find a way to make it up to me.

The next day, I called the Mayo clinic and spoke to the head oncologist over the radiation department. He told me that some people do experience dementia type symptoms due to the radiation, but it is only temporary. We did not know this could be a side effect of radiation and all this time I tried to help him, but I didn't know how to help. I want others to know this is a side effect that could happen to anyone with no warning signs. If we had known in the beginning, maybe I could have told Daniel he was being angry and we could have worked through it easier. It was really hard on me and he still doesn't remember the things he said to me that was so hurtful. I keep a journal and that is the only way I could express my feelings at the time. I couldn't speak to anyone else about it. I allowed Daniel to read through my journal after we discovered what was causing so much of his anger. He was in tears and told me he could not remember saying any of those things to me.

Our 5th wedding anniversary was November 29, 2023. I wanted us to be able to start over fresh after everything we had been through the last year. I wanted to put all the arguments, the cancer and the bad vibes between us in the past. I ordered us new wedding bands to celebrate a new beginning.

The night was a pink moon, a partial lunar eclipse and the Dracoid meteor shower. Under the beautiful sky I showed Daniel the new wedding bands. I explained why I chose to replace the ones from 5 years ago and he agreed to a new beginning for us. What better night to begin again than under the beauty of God's beautiful heaven's filled with shooting stars and a pink moon. We felt like that was the night destined for a new beginning ordained by God.

We are getting back to where we were before all the side effects, the emotions, the thought of dying and moving on towards a more beautiful and brighter future between the two of us.

I believe in learning from our past mistakes and applying them to the future. Our future is the only thing that matters.

Chapter 25

PSA numbers after 3 months

On December 5, 2023 we saw Daniel's urologist for blood work to check his PSA numbers. We walked into the office expecting the best outcome possible, but in the back of our minds we were both nervous. We know Daniel had carcinoma which is the type cancer that does not spread. Thank God it wasn't Metastasis which does spread. We know Daniel's urologist told us before the surgery that the cancer should never come back. It is still nerve wrecking to once again sit in the office.

We sat waiting for his name to be called trying to stay calm. After the blood work was taken, we drove home and took a nap. The night before we didn't sleep so well. The pressure was strong on us today as we prayed for the cancer to be cured and for the PSA numbers to show improvement. I knew Daniel was worried because he was being a grump after our nap. I told Daniel to look at his finger nails. He was showing vertical ridges on his nails. The oncologist told my mom a few months after her radiation that the ridges were a good sign the radiation had done its job. I knew I was trying to be soothing to him, but I also knew in the back of his mind was fear.

On the morning of December 6, I received the report from Labcorp in an email with the results of his blood work. We both held our breaths as I opened the report and began to read..... "OMG!" – I screamed as Daniel looked at me with terror on his face. I turned my phone to him so he could see the report for himself. At the very top it read his last PSA number was 14.9, but as of 12-5-23 his PSA number was 2.73. As tears trailed down our faces, he hugged me like never before. Thank God we both uttered while looking towards the heavens. I told him that is a huge reduction in his numbers and I am so proud of him. We were so excited we couldn't contain the news.

Daniel called Jay first, his older brother. Jay was ecstatic and screamed, "This is a wonderful day my brother". He told Daniel how proud he was of him and that Daniel was his hero. Jay admitted to Daniel that he was so afraid he would lose him and that was his greatest fear through the entire process. As tears were in the air both brothers said "I love you". What a miraculous feeling to be able to tell his brother such wonderful news after a year of worry.

Next we called Daniels parents. I had told them the previous day I would let them know as soon as I received the report. Daniel called his mom and she said his dad had asked several times if she had heard from me. They were on pins and needles to hear the results. We had them on speaker phone, just as they had us on speaker. I sent the report via text to mom and she opened it and they both said "Thank God". With such excitement we could hear the catch of emotions in their voices. The same catch in their voices as before, but this time it was great news.

Next we called Daniels younger brother, David. He reacted the same way with emotions in his voice. He spoke with such relief hearing the news. David hasn't been through losing someone he loved before like a brother. The entire situation was a new experience I don't think he will ever forget.

I feel for the first time in the past year, the entire family will sleep peacefully tonight. Daniel told me he still feels like he's in a haze. Going through everything he has in the past year and now having the numbers being so low is such a relief. Everyone is at ease and awe tonight. What a glorious weight lifted from our shoulders and our minds.

At the moment he is said to be in remission. After 5 years of remission he will be considered cancer free. We will see Daniel's urologist every

3 months for a while to keep a check on his numbers. Daniel's urologist told us the PSA numbers may creep up a tiny bit before they fall again, but that is normal. They should steadily keep going down to around one.

∽ Chapter 26 ∽
Conclusion

A cancer diagnosis hits you like a freight train to the brain. We had no idea what to expect and what was to come. The fear of the unknown is the most horrifying part to face. We both feel our laughter and trying to keep things as normal as possible in our lives helped us a lot. We chose to be "blissfully ignorant" and not worry every second of the day about what we had to face. Some felt we were not being serious about the diagnosis, but you must handle things the way you know best. Whatever is going to happen is happening whether you spend your days sad or if you spend your days celebrating life together and not wasting a moment of time.

You feel as if you have no control over your life, but certain aspects you can still control and that gives you power. We chose to control who we wanted to tell and when. We chose to be around only the people who were optimistic and avoid those who were negative. The more you choose to control within the situation, gives you a sense of peace. Your attitude is one thing you can control and this is not the time to think negatively or to waste your time being miserable. Of course, we spent time crying together when we needed to release emotions and that is perfectly normal. We tried not to allow it to consume our every thoughts.

As hard as a cancer diagnosis is to comprehend, it is even harder the way some people treat you. They are sad in the beginning and think your dying, some simply disappear and you learn who your true friends are during times like this. You will hear people telling you stories of their cancer journey, but the important thing to remember is that each patient is different. Each will have different symptoms and side effects and of course, some will say they breezed through with no side effects. I feel those are the people who are embarrassed to tell you what they actually experienced. As you can tell from these chapters, we are not embarrassed to tell what we encountered. We chose to try and help others to know the truth and to share the things we found that helped us make it to the other side.

I did not realize that the patient and others around you will go through the 5 stages of grief. Daniel's parents went through these stages, just as Daniel did. At the time, with so much on my mind I did not realize what was happening.

The 5 stages of grief are as follows:

1. **Denial** – When you first learn of an illness or a loss of a loved one, it's common to think "This isn't happening to me". You feel shocked or numb. This is a temporary way to deal with overwhelming emotions and a natural defense mechanism.

2. **Anger** – As reality sets in you are faced with the pain, frustration and helplessness. These thoughts turn into anger and often are directed towards loved ones, a higher power (like God), or life in general.

3. **Bargaining** – This stage you dwell on what you could have done to prevent the situation. Usually this is where prayer comes in trying to make a deal with God or a higher power.

4. **Depression** – Sadness sets in and you begin to realize the effect on your life. Symptoms include crying, sleep issues, decreased appetite or sometimes over eating. You feel overwhelmed, lonely and regret.

5. **Acceptance** – The final stage of grief is when you accept reality and what is really happening to you. You still feel sad and emotional, but you decide to move forward and accomplish what you need to so your life can move forward.

Most know these 5 stages when dealing with the loss of a loved one, but that isn't necessarily true. These 5 stages can be associated with many things such a devastating diagnosis. Some people may skip stages or experience them in a slightly different order.

I can now see looking back that Daniel's parents went through these stages. They felt helpless and they didn't realize what was happening subconsciously and being projected outward.

I can also see now that Daniel was going through the same thing. I now understand where his anger came from, but I feel it also came from the radiation. He still doesn't remember the hurtful things he said to me during the radiation process. Now that we have learned more about why these things were happening, we have found a way to move past it.

Daniel later confided in me where some of the anger came from months after the last treatment. I think all men can understand the reason behind this anger. He felt I would not see him as the same man because he wasn't producing semen. If you feel like this, don't assume how your partner might feel about this situation. Have a heart to heart conversation with them and be totally honest about how you feel. Your partner should not see you any differently than they did before the diagnosis. Remember a lot of times this side effect is only temporary.

I seem to experience "Delayed Grief". This type of grief is where you don't process all of your feeling at the time, but it becomes apparent weeks or months later. I feel I was trying so hard to keep Daniel in a good place mentally that I couldn't fully process my feelings until after it was over. I have been that way most of my life. Especially when I am the care giver trying to keep the other person mentally stable. Everything came flooding back like a tsunami while watching America's Got Talent about a week after Daniel's last treatment. Care givers often experience Delayed Grief because they spend their time being strong for their loved one.

You will also come across people who constantly tell you prostate cancer is the easiest to treat and you have nothing to worry about. Daniel and I became so tired of hearing those words that we wanted to scream. I know these people are trying to make you feel better, but until they are diagnosed with cancer they can't understand what a mental torture it is to deal with the situation. I feel people will say odd things that are sometimes offensive because they don't know how to respond to the situation.

I hope by sharing our experience with you this book will help cancer patients if only in a tiny way.

We learned so much throughout the process and we wanted to pass it on to others. May our new found knowledge help you in your treatment process and make it a bit easier. I included dates to show the time periods between different phases of treatments. We have also setup an email where you can contact us with your questions or if you need a sympathetic ear. The email address is at the beginning of this book.

Daniel and I send our sincerest love and prays to anyone going through cancer, those who are care givers, family members, and the thousands of cancer survivors.

May God surround you in his white light of healing and protection as you deal with the tribulations placed before you.

Photos from the Hope Bell Ceremony

A Note from Elizabeth

Things are very serious with most of the patients you meet at the cancer center. We made parachute bracelets and gave them out as a sign of being connected and offering support to other's who may not have anyone supporting them. Many times when we offered a bracelet to a patient it was greeted with a smile, tears and excepted with a huge hug.

I decided to try and make the staff smile when it was Daniel's turn for his treatment. The staff would pull his pants down to his hips so they could see the markers. His undercarriage was covered by his pants and underwear. Below is a few of the images I drew on Daniel near the markers to make the staff smile.

A Note from Daniel

I was going along living life feeling as everything was going great. When I found out cancer was lurking inside my body, I felt like everything I knew about myself was false. Apparently, the cancer cells had been inside my body for some time and I had no knowledge of the intruder inside me. I had no time to learn to deal or prepare for the fight I had ahead of me. I felt like I had been sucker punched in the head.

A cancer diagnosis knocks you down physically and emotionally. How you choose to handle it is up to you. That is one area of control you still have over your body. The most important thing at this moment is to get up and fight for your life. You only have two choices, first you can choose denial or you can choose life. The strongest emotions I felt was shame and weakness. As a man, the weakness of dealing with something like this is horrifying, but you must do what needs to be accomplished to make it to the other side.

More than anything I didn't want my wife to suffer through this with me. I would apologize to her for putting her through this, but she would tell me to stop apologizing because it could have been either of us with a cancer diagnosis.

I had no idea how dark my days could become. I would like for men to learn from my mistakes of arguing with my wife. I still do not remember most of the arguments. Cancer consumes not only your body, but also your mind. Try to be aware of the things you speak to each other. The most important lesson I learned is to keep an open line of communication because having someone to go through this with is paramount. Especially after reading our experiences your partner can bring to your attention that you are not handling things so well. Trust me some days are harder than others and some are very dark. You will struggle to make it on your own some days, but have the courage to make it to what lies on the other side.

I owe my life to my wife, Elizabeth. Without her it would have seemed impossible. At times, I didn't deserve her unyielding love and pure devotion. She helped me find my way through one of the hardest ordeals of my life.

Research your doctors and put your trust in the one's you choose. They are your salvation incarnate. They care more than a lot of people think they do. My doctor's didn't see me as just another patient, but they saw Elizabeth and I as a couple going through a very difficult time. I couldn't have asked for a better team to treat me.

Elizabeth Jordan

In memory of my parents and our Canadian Lynx

Ruth & James Shores

Hannah

Another Book by Elizabeth Jordan

The Darkness of My Shattered Heart
Aug 31, 2016 at 8:03am ·

Book review by Eishinas

A Treasured read, close to heart

By: Eishinas on august 18, 2016
Format: Kindle Edition

Author Elizabeth Jordan should be honored and looked up-to-for her courage and ability to live as a fighter amidst turmoils and hardships thrown by destiny in her pathways of life.
"The Darkness of my shattered heart" is a heart wrenching yet inspiring memoir of author Elizabeth Jordan where she has captured some of the most depressing moments of loss and pain in her life. Author Elizabeth's memoir has created a special bond of respect and love in my heart towards her, and brought outbursts of emotions in me when I learnt how she suffered with the grief of losing her boyfriend at a very young age of 16 and when things were getting back to normal death of 'Caleb' made it really difficult for me to fight back my tears.
It was very thoughtful of author to write her memoir in a very natural and gripping style dividing this touching read into two parts, first half-the true incidents experienced by author and the other half-is a compilation of some of the most meaningful and motivational poems poured on paper by a suffered soul.
I am sure author Elizabeth is the chosen one by god for her inner strength and abilities to cope up with the negativity and yet to stand strong as an inspiration for other suffering beings. "The darkness of my shattered heart" is truly a treasured read I will hold close to my heart for its reality and courage.
I highly recommend this book to one and all.